ƒORGIVING

GOD

a

woman's

struggle

to

understand

when God

answers

no

ƒORGIVING

GOD

Carla Killough McClafferty

Discovery House Publishers is affiliated with
RBC Ministries, Grand Rapids, Michigan 49512

Discovery House books are distributed to the trade by
Thomas Nelson Publishers, Nashville, Tennessee 37214

Library of Congress Cataloging-in-Publication Data

McClafferty, Carla Killough, 1958–
    Forgiving God : a woman's struggle to understand
when God answers no / Carla Killough McClafferty.
      p. cm.

    ISBN 0-929239-97-0

    1. Consolation. 2. Grief—Religious aspects—
Christianity. 3. Bereavement—Religious aspects—
Christianity. 4. Children—Death—Religious aspects—
Christianity. 5. Spiritual healing. 6. McClafferty, Carla
Killough, 1958– . I. Title.
BV4907.M34   1995
248.8'6—dc20   95-16722
                            CIP

Dedication

I dedicate this book to my mother, Maxine Rucker Killough, and to the memories of my son, Corey Andrew Killough McClafferty, and my father, Raymond Francis Killough.

My mother has shown me a compassionate heart, generosity, and unconditional love throughout my life.

My son, about whom this book was written, gave me love, joy, and a deeper understanding of God.

My father, who died before the completion of this book, gave me strength, confidence, and curiosity.

Thank you.

Grace teaches us, in the midst of life's greatest comforts, to be willing to die, and, in the midst of its greatest crosses, to be willing to live.

Matthew Henry

Chapter 1

CHILLS RACED UP MY SPINE and my eyes filled with tears as Patti Tolliver, a new friend, told me about the death of her baby daughter in a car accident. Waves of grief washed over her, as overpowering at that moment as they were three years earlier when it happened. When I was able to speak I said, "I didn't know. I'm so sorry."

Seeing such heartache, I knew there was nothing I could say to comfort her. As I left, I regretted that our conversation had brought back her grief, raw and fresh.

Thoughts of Patti and her tragedy kept coming back to me. She must be stronger than I to be able to go on with her life. I thanked God for my three children and prayed that He would not let it happen in my own life. I knew in my heart that if one of my children died, I could not survive it. I loved them too much to live without any one of them.

On that sunny spring day, I didn't know that in only a few months I would find out for myself how a mother survives the loss of her child.

Chapter 2

IT WAS TO BE A THANKSGIVING that would change our lives forever. The day before was busy with errands, shopping, and cooking. My parents, Raymond and Maxine Killough, had arrived for the holidays and had taken our children Ryan, seven, Brittney, three, and Corey, fourteen months, into the backyard to play while I cooked supper.

I soon heard Corey cry, and stopped what I was doing. I started toward the door to see what was wrong, and met my mother in the dining room, holding him in her arms.

"He fell off the swing," she said.

Corey looked me in the eyes and reached for me. As soon as he was in my arms, he passed out. Panic gripped me as I realized something terrible was wrong.

I ran to the phone and called 911. Frantically I gave them the address and said, "My son fell off the swing and he is unconscious! Hurry, please hurry."

After dialing the number where my husband, Pat, worked I gave the phone to my father, then ran to the front yard, with Corey in my arms.

While I paced around waiting for an ambulance, I called "Corey, wake up. You've got to wake up."

My mother brought a wet rag, and as I bathed his face, she cried, "Carla, wake him up! Carla, wake him up!"

"I can't wake him up," I cried.

For what seemed like hours, I paced and cried and called to him to wake up. Then I realized his breathing pattern had changed. He was breathing harder than normal. An emergency medical technician in a police car finally arrived.

"He fell off the swing, then passed out," I blurted out.

"Did he lose consciousness immediately?" he asked as he took Corey out of my arms and put him in the back seat of the police car.

"No, it was about two minutes later," I explained, getting in on the other side.

"Did he vomit?"

"No."

While the EMT checked the pupils of his eyes, I noticed that Corey's breathing was still labored.

"How are his pupils?" I asked.

"Dilated and uneven."

I knew enough about head injuries to know that was not good. Corey vomited when they moved him from the police car to the ambulance. That was another bad sign.

My mother stayed with Ryan and Brittney while my father and I rode in the ambulance. Above the sound of the siren, I cried and prayed, *Dear Lord, help him. Let him be all right.*

On the way to the hospital, Corey cried out twice but didn't waken. The attendant said, "That's a good sign. He's going to be all right." I continued to pray.

Chapter 3

AFTER THE EMERGENCY ROOM doctor
checked Corey, I requested that a neurosurgeon be called in to see him. By the time Pat
arrived, Corey was lying on a stretcher,
stripped down to a diaper, and hooked up to
oxygen. He looked so small and helpless. He
lay still except for an occasional muscle
spasm that would cause one arm to stiffen. A
pallor had taken the place of his usual dark
complexion. I called the church office to re-
quest prayer for him.

While we waited for the neurosurgeon to
arrive, I thought back on the events of the

---

day. After Ryan left for school, Brittney, Corey, and I started our full day of errands. I had picked out the photographs I wanted to buy from a recent photo shoot of Corey. The photographer took twice as many poses as usual the day they were made and they all turned out well.

I told the pushy sales person, "I would love to have all of these pictures, but today I'll only buy the package deal."

The salesman said, "They sure are cute, you had better not pass them up."

I replied, "There will be lots of cute pictures of him I can buy in the future." While we were out shopping, I bought Corey some new shoes.

After their lunch and naps, Brittney and Corey were ready to help me cook. They pulled a chair up to their usual cooking spot at the sink. Equipped with bowls of water and wooden spoons, they began adding salt, pepper, and flour to their "soup." I worked around them and listened as they laughed and cooked. I stopped and watched them. It was one of those moments I wanted to hold on to. I got the camera to take a photograph, so I'd always remember how cute they looked.

With camera in hand, I said, "Look at me and smile." Since Corey loved to have his picture taken, he immediately shuffled his feet around on the chair to pose. As I focused the picture, I looked at the bruise on Corey's forehead where he had fallen on the patio the day before. He'd fallen on his head, cried for a minute, then after a kiss from Mom, forgot all about it.

I kissed each of their upturned faces and said, "I love you so much, and I'm thankful God gave you to me." I wanted to remember forever how adorable they looked. My mind's eye took in every detail of those few moments. The sweet smell of a baking cake, the dirty dishes piled in the sink, their delighted giggles as they added another spoonful of sugar to the "soup." I tucked the memory away in my heart along with many others.

About the time Ryan got out of school, my parents arrived. The kids wanted some of the pumpkin bread I had just taken from the oven. As Nana held Corey in her lap, he ate as much as he could hold, then started poking his fingers into the rest of the loaf.

My father said, "Corey, you don't need to punch holes in that."

Corey couldn't believe his Papa told him not to do something, and he began to cry. He climbed down from Nana's lap and stood there crying. I stopped what I was doing and knelt down beside him. He stopped crying and put his arms around me for a hug. He patted my back with one hand, the way he often did, and lifted his face for a kiss. I knelt there to hug and kiss as long as he wanted to. After a few minutes, he ran off to do something else.

I laughed and said, "That's the longest he has stayed still for hugs and kisses since he started walking."

Then Nana and Papa took the children outside. . . .

My attention was brought back to the emergency room when the neurosurgeon arrived. He examined Corey and said, "We need to get a C.T. scan immediately."

I am a Radiologic Technologist and I knew the technician doing the scan. While outwardly I made small talk with her, inside I was hysterical. She allowed me stay in the room with Corey during the scan. I wanted to be there when he woke up. I held his pacifier so that when he awakened I would have something that would comfort him.

During the scan I prayed over and over, *Lord, please wake him up and let him be all right.*

When the films were ready, Pat and I went in to talk to the doctor and look at them. Before the doctor said anything, my eyes searched the scans hanging on the view box. My heart lurched in my chest. I had seen enough C.T. scans to know what a normal one looked like. And I knew this one wasn't typical. The ventricle on the left side of his head didn't look normal.

The neurosurgeon said, "Corey's brain is swollen, causing the left ventricle to be displaced. The swelling will continue and should peak sometime within the next twenty-four to forty-eight hours. For example, when you have an ankle injury, it takes a while before the swelling gets to its fullest, then the swelling goes down. After the swelling in Corey's brain has peaked, he will either be fine, or he will have brain damage. We won't know the outcome until the swelling has peaked and Corey wakes up."

From far away, I heard my own voice say, "Isn't there some kind of surgery you can do?"

He said, "If there was a blood clot or pool of blood there, I could go in and remove it. But Corey doesn't have either of those. It is Corey's brain tissue that is swollen. There have been some studies done where they remove the skull to allow for the swelling, but they've found that there was no difference in the outcome of the patients who had this surgery compared to those who didn't."

"Is there another doctor or hospital anywhere in the world that could do something for him that cannot be done here?" I asked, knowing we would go anywhere to get help for him.

"There is nothing that can be done anywhere else that we can't do here," he said.

Everything seemed unreal, as if I had stumbled across a nightmare in progress. I couldn't believe this was really happening. This man was telling me that my perfect son could now be brain-damaged. It couldn't be; I was hugging and kissing him two hours ago. This reality was more horrible than any nightmare had ever been.

As my mind struggled to make sense of what was happening, I knew that if Corey were left with brain damage, I would do whatever it took to help him. I could learn how to help him. Together we could face anything. My love for him did not depend upon his mental or physical perfection. I would love him regardless of the outcome.

The doctor explained, "Corey will need to go to the Intensive Care Unit. We will begin medication to rid his body of excess fluid. The head of his bed will be elevated about thirty degrees. His electrolytes will be monitored to make sure they stay in balance."

I asked, "Will we need to do another C.T. scan to watch the progress?"

"No, we can follow his progress with neurological exams."

All we could do was wait and pray.

Chapter 4

COREY WAS TAKEN to the Intensive Care Unit. His breathing was normal, and his pupils were normal and reacting to light. They started an IV and put in a catheter. The nurse came in with the first dose of medication that would get rid of excess fluid.

"Is it possible to have an allergic reaction to this medication?" I asked.

"I've never heard of anyone reacting to this medication," she said.

Keeping a close watch on the amount of urine that collected in the catheter bag, I was encouraged to see that Corey was getting rid of a lot of fluid. The more fluid he lost, the less there would be to swell his brain.

Since I thought our hospital stay might be a long one, I made a list of clothes and things I wanted Pat to bring me from home. My sisters, Karen McGuire and Debbie Matlock, and their families came to see Corey.

As Pat left to get my things from home, he said, "He is going to be fine; don't worry."

When I walked out in the hall, a group from my church was waiting there. Their presence was a comfort to me. I was grateful for the concern and support they showed by coming to the hospital. I knew they would be praying for us.

Pat hadn't returned with my clothes yet when visiting hours were over. When everyone had gone, I looked down at Corey lying in the hospital bed. He was so small he didn't even make a dent in the mattress. I could barely breathe past the lump in my throat. I smoothed his hair and kissed him.

In the silence of the Intensive Care Unit, my whispered prayer sounded like a shout as I prayed, "Dear God, help us. We need you. I pray that you would protect his brain from damage. I know you can bring us through this without any lasting damage. Lord, please help him and wake him up."

I was encouraged when Corey began moving around a little. He was moving restlessly as if he were trying to wake up from a deep sleep. I thought if I talked to him, he would try harder to wake up. I patted him and said, "Corey, it is time to wake up. Ryan and Brittney want you to come home to play."

While watching him, I continued to talk, "I know you feel sleepy, but you have got to wake up now." I expected his eyes to open at any moment.

The nurse brought in a rocking chair and said, "You can hold him as long as you keep his head elevated."

Wanting so much to hold him in my arms, I maneuvered the IV pole in position to move with us to the rocking chair. I reached for the catheter bag, and my hand froze in midair. It was empty. Corey had not passed any urine since the last time it was emptied. I knew there should be urine in the bag, since he had an IV with medication in it to get rid of excess fluid. My knees shook as waves of fear washed over me.

Rocking in the chair with Corey in my arms I prayed, *Lord, I think he is trying to wake up. Thank you. I pray you would wake him up completely.*

I rocked, talked, and prayed. I said, "I love you so much. When we get home, we will read books and play. Everything is going to be all right."

As I had many times before, I kissed his nose and picked up his dimpled hand and put it on my cheek. I thought of all the times at home when I had held him in my arms, just like this, and watched him sleep. The dishes and clothes would wait, but my son wouldn't be a baby very long.

He looked as though he were asleep, but something was different. His muscles felt tense and stiff instead of relaxed. I checked the pupils of his eyes every few minutes to make sure they were reacting to light and weren't dilated. Deep inside, I knew the child I had gotten out of his crib that morning would never be the same.

It was 10:50 P.M. and Corey still had not awakened. I knew Pat would be back soon with my clothes from home. I looked down at Corey and saw that his face had begun to break out with red and white blotches. In the same instant, his breathing became labored. I pressed the call button and shrieked, "Corey's face has red and white blotches all over. Come quick!"

Don't panic, I told myself, maybe it's an allergic reaction to the medication.

As the nurse entered the room I said, "He was fine one second, and the next he was covered with blotches, and started breathing harder."

She bent down over Corey still in my arms and opened his eyelids. My heart hit the floor when I saw his pupils were dilated. She got out her light to test their reaction to light, but before she could check them, Corey stopped breathing.

Chapter 5

"HE'S NOT BREATHING!" I screamed as I carried him toward the bed.

"Lay him on the bed," she snapped over her shoulder as she called for the emergency team.

I stood there screaming as she began breathing for him with a bag. The emergency team came running in from all parts of the hospital. While they began working on him a woman led me to a small room nearby and stayed with me. I was hysterical, screaming and praying, "God, save him. Please save him. Help him, God." Over and over I prayed.

Through the haze I heard the woman say, "The doctors will save him, they can help him."

You don't understand, I thought. *God is the only one who can save him.*

At that moment, Pat was returning from home with my clothes, and he heard me screaming as he came down the hall.

After I told him what happened, Pat called my parents and sisters. My parents and Gary, my brother-in-law, stayed at home with all of our children. Karen and Debbie, my sisters, and Debbie's husband, Ronnie, came to the hospital.

For an hour and a half, there was no word. All we could find out was that they were still with Corey. Time seemed to stand still as my mind frantically rehearsed all the things that could be happening. Had his heart stopped? Were they shocking his heart, even as I sat there? Were they still having to breathe for him? Was it an allergic reaction to the medicine? Was the code team still working to get him to breathe on his own? Was he dead? I waited and wondered and prayed, *God, save him. God, please save him.*

This can't be happening. I felt a sense of unreality, as if I were acting out a part in a bad TV show. It was too horrible to be true, yet I knew it was. It was no longer a matter of whether or not Corey would have brain damage. I knew my son could die.

The doctor came out and said, "We put in a nasal gastric tube, an arterial line, and put him on a respirator. While this episode is not a good sign, technically, Corey isn't much worse than he was before. He didn't go without oxygen, and his reactions are about the same as they were before. He can breathe on his own when the respirator is turned off."

"Could this have been an allergic reaction to the medication?" I asked.

"I feel sure it was not a reaction to medication, but even if it was, we have no choice but to continue to give it to him."

The hours that followed proved him right; it was not an allergic reaction.

Chapter 6

A NURSE STAYED IN THE ROOM with us to monitor Corey's condition throughout the night. The arterial line put in place earlier was used by the lab to draw blood to test his electrolytes and blood gases. The nurse periodically checked his pupils' reactions to light and ran a pen up his foot to check his reaction to a stimulus.

Pat and I sat by Corey's bed and watched him, too stunned to talk. I saw Corey's face break out with blotches again. Since he was hooked up to monitors, I saw his heart rate and blood pressure suddenly go higher. The nurse checked his pupils.

"Are they dilated again?" I asked.

"Yes."

If he hadn't been on the respirator, I knew he would have stopped breathing again. My knees felt like they had turned to jello.

After about fifteen minutes, Corey's heart rate, blood pressure, and pupils returned to normal. The staff felt these episodes were the result of swelling in his brain.

I prayed, *God, I'm asking you to save Corey's life. Even if he comes out of this with severe brain damage, please save him. Lord, don't let him die. I know the outcome is in your hands. You have said in your Word to ask and it shall be given you, seek and you shall find, knock and it shall be opened unto you. Lord, I'm asking, seeking, and knocking. I am asking with every shred of faith I have that you will save Corey's life. I believe that you can save him, and I believe that you will.*

The lab came and took the second blood sample to check on his electrolytes and blood gases. When the results came back, I asked how they looked.

"They are not as good as the first set."

Dear God, let his blood tests come back better next time. Help him to improve, I prayed.

Through the night, the pattern was the same. When the pressure would increase in Corey's brain, it set off the same chain of events. For about fifteen minutes his face broke out in blotches, his pupils dilated, and his heart rate and blood pressure soared. The respirator kept him breathing. Then everything would return to normal.

During these episodes, I would stroke Corey's silky cheek and wonder if the pressure was destroying his ability to see, hear, speak, walk, or move. Would I ever see that cheek dimple into a smile again? My son was in trouble and there was nothing I could do about it.

The third set of lab results came back. As the nurse read them, I prayed, *God, please let them be better than before.*

When she looked up, she saw the silent question on my face and said, "These are not as good as the second set."

The feeling of complete helplessness overwhelmed me. All I could do was pray,

---

and it seemed as though my prayers were going no higher than the ceiling.

Thinking back over my life, I confessed every sin I could think of, in case there was some sin in my life hindering my prayers. Again I prayed, *Dear God, I know Corey's life is in your hands. I pray you will have mercy on us and save Corey's life. Whatever the outcome of his mental condition, please don't let him die. Your Word says that 'whatever things you ask in prayer, believing, you shall receive.' Lord, I'm asking, and I believe you can save him and that you will save him.*

The next lab report was worse than the previous ones. Again I prayed, *God, I know you are in control. You can make a change for the better in his blood tests. Lord, I pray you would let there be some improvement in his blood work next time.*

Every time the lab tests were done, the results were not as good as the previous one. I knew by watching the nurse that Corey's reactions to light and stimuli were worse. As each hour passed, his condition deteriorated.

Everyone insisted that Pat and I lie down for a while. They took us to a room to rest. Even though I was numb with exhaustion, I couldn't sleep. I lay there and looked out the window at the predawn sky. While the sky began to brighten toward daybreak, I prayed, *Dear Lord, please help us. By medical standards, Corey seems to be getting worse. I know that you are the Great Physician. I know nothing is too hard for you, and you have the power to turn his condition around. I ask that you would protect Corey and heal him. It is almost dawn. Please let this be the turning point. I pray that with the rising sun, you would bring improvement in his condition. I believe you can and you will.*

When I couldn't stand to be away from Corey one more minute, I opened the door. Huddled together on the floor just outside the door were my two sisters and brother-in-law. I saw the worried look on their faces. I asked, "How is he?"

"He had another episode," they said.

Chapter 7

THANKSGIVING DAY DAWNED bright and clear, but with no improvement in Corey's condition. The staff insisted we get something to eat while the doctor examined Corey and the nurse's shift change was complete. I sat across the table from Pat in the cafeteria. I was unable to speak or get any food past the lump in my throat. I only wanted my son.

Remembering all I had ever learned about prayer, I asked myself again if anything in my life could be hindering my prayers. I forgave every trespass against me, confessed and asked forgiveness for my sins.

I prayed, *Holy Father in heaven, I come boldly to your throne of grace and ask for mercy. I ask that you would save Corey's life. I know that you are the Great Physician, and all things are possible with you. Your Word says with the faith of a grain of mustard seed, mountains can be moved. Your Word says to ask believing and it shall be done. You have said to ask, seek, knock and it shall be opened unto you. Lord, I'm praying with every bit of faith I have that you will save Corey's life. I know you are the only one who can save him, and I believe you will.*

Knowing God could save Corey no matter how weak his condition, I thought, that must be it! God will save Corey when there could be no doubt that God alone had saved him from death. Our situation will be a beautiful example of God's grace and power.

The doctor was still in with Corey when we returned from the cafeteria. Every few minutes I checked to see if they were done so I could go back in the room. He stayed with Corey for about an hour and a half. I wondered what was taking so long, and I continued to pray.

When the nurse came out she said, "The doctor wants to get another C.T. scan."

Since he had told us before that another scan was unnecessary, I thought he must be hoping there would be a change that he could do something about, like a pool of blood he could operate on.

When the doctor finished examining Corey, he came out to speak with us. He said, "Corey is not breathing for himself when the respirator is off. If the swelling has gotten worse, I'm afraid we are going to lose him."

"Do you mean he could die?" I asked.

"Yes."

I was stunned. He had put into words the fear that had been growing inside me through the long hours of the night. The fear I couldn't, and wouldn't, say aloud. With his answer ringing in my ears, it was no longer my unspoken fear, it was a real possibility.

We returned to Corey's bedside. When I saw Corey, I felt like I had been punched in the stomach and couldn't breathe. The change in him was unbelievable. He had dark circles under sunken eyes, as though he had been ill for months instead of just a few hours. I knew he was dying.

I prayed, *Dear Almighty God, I'm asking for a miracle. I beg you to spare his life. He is dying and only you can save him. Please don't let him die.*

During the C.T. scan I prayed, *Lord, I know you can save Corey. I pray the swelling isn't worse. Whatever condition he is left in, just don't let him die.*

The doctor came to get us after the scan. Solemnly, the three of us walked down the hall. The hospital was empty and silent that Thanksgiving morning. Halfway down the hall, I couldn't wait one more second and asked, "Is it worse?"

"Yes," he answered.

As we went into the film-viewing room, my eyes immediately went to the films hanging there. I could see the left side was worse than before and now the right side was swollen also. I felt sick. At last the doctor said, "Corey's kidneys are pouring urine now. I've never seen anyone survive when this happens."

I had to know. I began to speak, but my voice didn't sound like my own. It sounded empty somehow, empty and desolate. I asked, "How long does he have, days or hours?"

"Hours."

Chapter 8

BACK IN THE INTENSIVE CARE UNIT with Corey, Pat and I sat side by side and held our son. Our pastor, Tom Hart, came to be with us. I held Corey in my arms and cried. Without a word I tried to make sense out of what was happening. We watched in horror as his condition grew worse every minute. The pull of death was getting stronger.

I felt I had ice flowing through my veins. My heart was pounding as if it would explode. I felt empty. There was nothing we could do. There was no procedure, no doctor, no hospital in all the world that could make a difference. Corey's life was in God's hands. I continued to pray, *God, I beg of you to grant us a miracle. I know he is dying, but you can restore his life. I need him. I'll do anything, go anywhere, just don't let him die. If someone must die, take me instead. O God, hurry, he doesn't have much time.*

After I prayed this time, from somewhere deep in my soul, I realized God was not going to send a miracle. In that instant, I knew Corey was going to die.

Kissing the curve of his nose I said, "I love you."

Pat and I told him, "Don't give up, you must keep fighting. We love you."

I touched him from head to toe, wanting to memorize the way he felt. Picking up one chubby little foot, I realized that exactly twenty-four hours earlier we were buying his new shoes. Was it only yesterday that my life was normal? It seemed so long ago. I kissed Corey's foot and remembered how patiently he'd tried on one shoe after the other. I smiled when I thought of the sweet smile he flashed me when we'd decided on a pair. As

I touched his toes, I knew he would never run and play in those new shoes. We would never search under beds and in the toy box for one missing shoe as we dressed to leave the house.

I held him tighter and tighter as if I could keep death away from him. His life was slipping away no matter how tightly I held him. I knew God was calling Corey out of our home into His heavenly home. Crying, I said, "No, no, no."

I thought, *I'm not going to let you die, I won't let God take you away from me.* I fought for him with all my strength. I prayed, *Oh God, where are you? Don't you hear me? Please do something before it is too late. I beg you not to take him away from me. I need him more than you do. I can't live without him. Don't take him away from me, he needs me and I need him. He is only a baby, he needs his mother. Please don't take my baby from me.*

Even as I wrestled with God to keep Corey alive, I felt Corey's spirit leaving his body. I don't know how, but I knew it and felt it. I saw Jesus sitting on a throne at the right hand of God. I couldn't see His face but I knew it was Jesus. He stood up and stretched out his arms toward us. He accepted Corey's spirit into heaven. It lasted only a second or two, and no one else in the room saw anything. In that fleeting instant, I felt Jesus' love for me and compassion for my breaking heart. Without words, it was as if He were telling me, "My dear child, I know you don't understand, just trust Me."

Nothing in the room had changed. I heard the swoosh of the respirator as it continued to breathe for Corey. His heart rate and blood pressure were very low. He looked and felt the same. I fought to keep him but I couldn't stop death from snatching him from my arms.

I knew Corey's spirit was in heaven, safe in the arms of Jesus. I held his body, and Jesus held his spirit.

Eternity had begun for Corey while I held him in my arms. I hugged him and wondered, what if he were dying because he needed a liver or kidney? What if he had been born with a disease, and needed an organ transplant to survive? Was there another mother somewhere watching helplessly as her child dies? For that mother, the only hope for her child is for another child to die. What if that had been our circumstance? If Corey needed a new heart or liver, would I pray that a mother would find it in her heart to give him a chance at life even when it meant her own child had died?

Gently, I opened Corey's eyelids and looked into his big brown eyes. The only one of our children with brown eyes like his father, I thought about how expressive his eyes had always been. His eyes always mirrored his thoughts, full of interest when he searched his favorite book to find the picture of a kitty. They twinkled with mischief when he knocked over the stack of towels I had just folded. They were soft with love when I rocked him to sleep. Now they were empty and unseeing.

I wondered if there was a child some-where who had never seen his or her moth-er's face because of the need for a cornea transplant.

We could make a difference in the lives of people. Corey's life on earth was over, but through him other children could have a chance at a fuller life.

"Do you think we should donate his or-gans?" I asked Pat.

"Yes," he answered.

In my heart I knew Corey's spirit was al-ready with Jesus, but I had to know whether or not he was brain-dead. I had to know in my own mind that without a doubt, there was absolutely no chance for his survival before we made a final decision about organ dona-tion.

We asked the pediatrician to come in and said, "We are considering donating Corey's organs. But before we make the decision, we want to get an electroencephalogram (EEG) done to see if there is any brain activity."

"We will get one." he said.

———

The young man arrived to perform the EEG. With tears in his eyes he explained, "Corey's body temperature is too low right now to do the test. We must get his body temperature up to at least ninety-five degrees before we can begin." I nodded my head, unable to speak. I was touched by the compassion I saw in his face, realizing that he was the first employee who had shown any emotion.

During the EEG I prayed, *Lord, I know Corey's spirit is with you. But it isn't too late, for nothing is too hard for the Lord. I pray you would give him back to me even now. Let this test show lots of brain activity. There are people watching who would witness your mighty power if you would let him survive. They would have no doubt that you had granted a miracle. Dear God, send him back to me. I am begging you. Please have mercy on us and save him. Please send me a miracle, and I'll never stop praising your name, and giving you the glory.*

The doctor came out. He sat down and said, "I pronounced him dead at 2:32 P.M. There was no brain activity."

Pat and I returned to Corey's room. For the last time, I picked my son up out of bed. I held him in my arms and said, "My darling Corey, I love you so much." His spirit was already gone and the doctor had pronounced him dead, but I could still hear the swoosh, swoosh of the respirator as it breathed for him. His physical body was deteriorating with each passing moment.

I held him in my arms and cried, "No, no, no." This time I was not fighting off death, but rather refusing to believe this was really happening.

It was over. We held Corey and told him how much he meant to us. Now it was time to leave. I lay him down for the last time. I smoothed his hair, touched his skin and kissed him. I left the room with the swoosh of the respirator echoing in my ears.

We signed the papers to allow Corey's corneas, heart, kidneys, and liver to be used for transplants. We were told we would never know who received his organs, and the recipient would never know who the donor was.

The only information we would get would be sketchy details such as the age, sex, and city where the transplant was done.

Pat and I drove home in silence. Questions rolled and tumbled around in my mind. How could my healthy son be dead? How could I live without him? How will I get out of bed each day knowing he won't be there? How could we tell a seven- and a three-year-old that their brother was dead? How can I explain it to them when I don't understand it myself? How will this affect them? Didn't you hear me? Where are you, God?

Chapter 9

IT WASN'T A SLOW REALIZATION that he was gone, but an instantaneous remembrance of every detail when I wakened from a fitful sleep the next morning. I strained to hear the rustle of Corey's sheets and the sound of his voice, knowing I would never hear it again.

Corey had always been the first one in the house to awaken. I woke up each morning at the first rustle of his bed sheets. I would lie in bed and listen while he played and talked to himself. I enjoyed listening to his baby talk and knew he would outgrow this phase quickly. I made a point to preserve in my memory the tranquillity of the early mornings, and the peace of knowing all my children were safe in their beds. I would lie there until he was ready to get out of his crib. When I entered his room each morning, he greeted me with a dazzling smile and reached out his arms for me.

Only forty-eight hours ago Corey was reaching out for me, eager to begin the day.

This morning was different. The void left by Corey's death was consuming. Not only could I feel the void, I could hear it, smell it, taste it, and see it. I would give everything I had for one more day with him, one more smile.

The thought that I still had two children who needed me now more than ever forced me out of bed. This was the first day of the rest of my life without my precious son. There were things that must be done.

I packed Corey's clothes for the last time. A new outfit Nana had given him, socks, his new shoes, and a diaper. The thought filtered through my mind that he wouldn't need a diaper, but I took one anyway.

With his clothes in a paper bag, Pat and I went to make the funeral arrangements. On the ride there and back, I couldn't believe people were coming and going as if nothing had happened. Didn't they know my son was dead? How could the world go on as if everything were normal, when it would never be normal again? The sun came up as it always had. The world around us was continuing, but our world was shattered.

After the horror of picking out a casket and making the funeral arrangements, I felt I didn't want to see him at the funeral home. I thought if I didn't see Corey lying in a casket, I would remember him in life rather than in death. Two people encouraged me to reconsider that decision. Carolyn Jones had lost a ten-year-old daughter; Brenda Martin, a newborn son. They felt it was important to see one's child in death. They wanted me to think carefully about it and make the decision that was right for me. They knew that soon it would be too late and I would always live with my decision. I will be forever grateful for that advice. I changed my mind and decided I did want to see him at the funeral home.

For me, it was the right decision. Pat and I said goodbye to him together, and each of us did so privately. We had brought Corey into this life together, and together we saw him leave it.

Chapter 10

THE TIME CAME when Ryan returned to school, Pat returned to work, and my parents went home. The funeral was behind us and everyone went back to a normal routine. Fewer calls and cards came. The state of shock that surrounded me for the first couple of weeks began to wear off and cold, hard reality set in.

Knowing I could not see or touch Corey filled me with despair. I knew I would be with Corey in eternity, but how could I possibly get through the rest of my life here without him? It seemed I had fallen into a black hole of misery so deep my screams of grief were without sound. A place so sad, my tears ran dry. A place so empty, I could not pray. A place so bitter, I didn't want to pray.

Memories were everywhere. There was not a nook or cranny in the house that Corey had not investigated. Every household chore I did brought a wave of agony. Since I was a stay-at-home mom, he was with me every minute of the day. He was always within arm's reach or in my sight. My heart hurt, my soul hurt, and I felt shaky all the time. It was as if my body were going through a withdrawal from not being able to touch him.

While Ryan was at school, Brittney and I wandered around the house not knowing what to do. Too young at barely three years old to put her grief into words, she would cry for long periods of time. When she cried, we would sit in the rocker and cry together.

While Brittney talked about Corey all day long, Ryan wouldn't talk about him at all. I worried that he was keeping it bottled up inside him. My heart was shattered, not only for myself, but for my children, husband, and parents as well. I did my best to figure out *why.* Why did God give Corey to us and then let him die at fourteen months of age?

I had been surprised but delighted when I'd discovered I was pregnant again when Ryan was five and Brittney was fourteen months old. From the beginning, I felt God had a special purpose in mind for Corey. But why would God allow Corey to die as a baby if He had a special plan for his life? Why didn't He let Corey grow up and fulfill the mission He had planned for him?

One day as I was talking to my best friend, Darlene Shelton, I said, "I always felt God had a special purpose for Corey's life. I thought he would grow up to be a preacher, maybe a missionary, or be in the right place at the right time to prevent a catastrophe, or save someone's life. Now he won't grow up to do any of those things."

"Carla," she said, "just think, that is exactly what he has done. He has saved several lives through the donation of his organs."

I had never dreamed that saving someone else's life would mean that his must
come to an end.

Chapter 11

OVER AND OVER I WONDERED why God didn't answer my prayers to save Corey's life. Didn't He hear me? Was He too busy to listen? Didn't He care that my son was dying? Was it an accident that God had no control over? Did God take the life of my child as a punishment for some sin? What kind of God would take an innocent child's life as a punishment? I knew God had the power to save Corey's life, yet He'd turned a deaf ear to my prayers and refused. The God I had loved and worshipped turned his back on me when I needed Him the most.

If a child had to die, why did God take my son? Why didn't He take the life of a child who was being abused or neglected? A child who could have been spared a childhood of torment and sorrow? If God had set out to punish someone by taking the life of a child, why didn't He take one from an atheist? Or a child from someone who had previously given away or aborted a child? If I had done something like that in my life perhaps I could have understood, but I'd lived my life trying to do what was right in the eyes of God. I wanted each of my children and was grateful for them. I took my children to church and taught them to love and serve God. I couldn't find any justice in this.

I kept thinking of the verses in my Bible that I'd highlighted so long ago. "Ask, and it will be given to you; seek, and you will find; knock, and it will be opened to you" (Matthew 7:7).

"Whatever things you ask in prayer, believing, you will receive" (Matthew 21:22).

"Jesus answered and said to them, 'Have faith in God. For assuredly, I say to you, whoever says to this mountain, "Be removed and be cast into the sea," and does not doubt in his heart, but believes that those things he says will be done, he will have whatever he says. Therefore I say to you, whatever things you ask when you pray, believe that you receive them, and you will have them' " (Mark 11:22–24).

Weren't these promises from God? I believed these verses with all my heart, so why didn't God do what He said He would do? I had always believed that God never broke a promise, but now I didn't know what to believe. I remembered every prayer I had prayed from the moment of Corey's accident. Why didn't God answer my prayers? Was it me? Didn't I have enough faith to save my son? Was there a grain of unbelief in my heart I didn't know about that canceled out my prayers? Was there not one among my family and church who had enough faith for their prayers to be answered?

All I had were questions, but I couldn't find satisfactory answers for any of them. I didn't know what to believe anymore. I doubted everything I had ever believed about God. The only thing I didn't doubt was that Corey was in heaven and that I will go there too because I had accepted Jesus as my Savior years before.

"We know that all things work together for good to those who love God, to those who are the called according to His purpose" (Romans 8:28). When tragedy happens, this verse is often quoted by people trying to bring comfort to a grieving family. Yet, I found no comfort there. When someone quoted this verse to me, I would nod my head and wonder how good they thought things would be if their son were dead, instead of mine. I felt it was a comforting verse only if the tragedy is in someone else's life.

What could be good about my son's death? Except for the fact that Corey's organs had given life to other children, I could see no good in any of it. Maybe something good could have come from it if someone had witnessed God's power to save Corey from death. By witnessing the power of prayer, their lives could perhaps be changed. But now, instead of praising God, I felt betrayed and angry. Nothing good could come from the way I felt toward God now.

There was no end to the pain. It seemed that every week something would happen that caused more heartache.

I answered the phone one day and a woman said, "This is the hospital. I see by our records that Corey is fifteen months old now. I'm calling to remind you it is time for him to have his MMR shot."

"Corey died last month," I managed to say.

Another time when I answered the phone, a woman said, "I am calling from the anesthesiologist's office to inform you that if you do not pay your bill immediately, we will turn this account over to a collection agency." Not really understanding everything she said I replied, "But we have already paid all the hospital bills."

"Well, this one has not been paid," she snapped.

"What was the date on the bill?" I asked.

"November 24, last year," she said.

"What test did you say this bill was for?"

"This bill is for anesthesiology service," she tossed back.

White-hot fury flowed through my veins when I realized she was trying to collect on the expenses for the organ retrieval surgery. Those expenses are paid for by the organ retrieval organization, not the donor's family.

"Lady, don't you ever call me again. Those are expenses paid for by ARORA. We allowed our son's organs to be used for transplanting and you have the audacity to call me about the bill," I screamed.

"Well," she stuttered, "I saw ARORA on here, but I didn't know what it meant."

"Did you ever think about finding out what it meant before calling me? It stands for Arkansas Regional Organ Recovery Agency. You call the director over there and don't you dare call me again," I shouted, then slammed down the receiver.

I was crying and shaking with anger at this woman's mistake, and angry with ARORA for not making sure this kind of thing did not happen.

Just more proof that God had deserted me and would not shield me from even the slightest pain.

Chapter 12

BEFORE COREY'S DEATH, there weren't enough hours in the day to do everything, now it seemed there were too many hours. I forced myself out of bed every day wishing it were over. I knew that for the rest of my life I would wake up and Corey would still be dead.

Corey, Corey, Corey. I couldn't think of anything else. The accident, the ambulance, the hospital, the prayers, the organ donation, the funeral. Over and over it played in my mind. Like a movie playing twenty-four hours a day, when it got to the end, it would rewind and start all over.

God seemed far from me. I couldn't feel His presence as I used to. Every day I drifted further and further away from Him. I was too weak to pray, and sadly found I didn't even want to pray anymore.

Prayers wouldn't do me any good now. My son was dead and my faith died with him. My thoughts were so blasphemous I couldn't share them with anyone. Deep in my heart, I couldn't forgive God for letting Corey die. Before Corey died, I tried to live my life in a way that was pleasing to God. And yet, when I really needed God, He'd abandoned me.

How could I ever go to church again and hear how God's will and timing is perfect, that He never makes a mistake? I didn't want to hear it when I couldn't believe it anymore.

As days grew into weeks I continued to be angry at God and felt guilty about it. I had been taught that it was wrong to question God, but now all I could do was question Him.

There seemed to be a tug-of-war within me over the direction my life should go. Like a pathetic comedy routine on TV, it seemed I had a little devil sitting on one shoulder and an angel on the other. The devil shouted in my ear the things that were easy to believe. Loud and clear I could hear him say, *You trusted God and look where it's gotten you. God could have saved Corey's life but He let him die. He turned a deaf ear to all your prayers and let you down when you needed Him most. What kind of God is that?*

The angel on the other shoulder was harder to hear and easier to ignore. He spoke in a still, small voice saying, *Trust God.*

I was conscious of the invisible but very real spiritual warfare taking place around me. I began to see how cunning the devil is. The devil couldn't get my soul, but he could keep me in such confusion and misery it could cause me to turn my back on God. I knew how much influence I had over my two small children. If I turned from God now, would either of my children ever accept Jesus as their personal Savior?

During the times when I felt I couldn't make it one more minute, that I would die of a broken heart, I could hear a still, small voice from within say, "I know." I knew God was telling me, *I know how hurt and confused you are. I know you don't understand. Trust Me and remember that I watched as My son died too.*

The hymn "Turn Your Eyes Upon Jesus" began going through my mind at unexpected times. Though this song had never had any particular meaning to me before, now the words came to me over and over as if to comfort me.

Turn your eyes upon Jesus,
Look full in His wonderful face:
And the things of earth will grow
    strangely dim
In the light of His glory and grace.[*]

Chapter 13

ONE DAY A LITTLE PACKAGE CAME in the mail. Enclosed was a copy of *Death of a Little Child* by J. Vernon McGee. I put it on the bookshelf without reading it. About two weeks later, I looked at the envelope and saw it was postmarked from Fayetteville, Arkansas. There wasn't a return address on it. Our name, house number, and street were correct, but it had the name of our town plus Little Rock on it. The zip code was incorrect. The booklet was inside with a blank sheet of paper wrapped around it. There was no note, signature, or any indication of who had sent it. We did not know anyone in Fayetteville. As confusing as the address was, I was surprised it reached us at all. I supposed someone must have read the obituary in the newspaper and gotten our address from there. Yet, it seemed odd to me that they wouldn't include some sort of a note with it. When I read this short booklet, the following passage spoke directly to my troubled heart.

A Brief Life Is Not an Incomplete Life

We sometimes feel that a life which was so brief was in vain, and that God has mocked us by giving us the little one and then by taking it away immediately. The child had no opportunity to perform a work, nor was there any time given to develop character. Let us remember, first of all, that the little one had an eternal spirit, and that it has gone into the presence of God where there will be an eternity to perform works and develop character.

With eternity as a measuring rod, the long life of Methuselah was merely a pinpoint on the calendar of time. Although the span of life of your little one was brief, it completed a mission, served a purpose and performed a God-appointed task in this world. Its presence turned your thoughts to the best, its helplessness brought out your strength and protection, and its loveliness roused your tenderness and love. Its influence will linger in your heart as long as you live. If anything can bring a man to God, it is a child. "A little child shall lead them" is not idle rhetoric. We think of Methuselah in connection with old age, but did you ever consider him as an infant? Well, he was once a baby and a most arresting thing is recorded about his birth. He was the son of Enoch, and it is written: "And Enoch lived sixty and five years, and begat Methuselah: and Enoch walked with God after he begat Methuselah three hundred years, and begat sons and daughters: and all the days of Enoch were three hundred sixty and five years: and Enoch walked with God: and he was not; for God took him" (Genesis 5:21–24). We do not know what the life of Enoch was for the first sixty-five years, but when the day came that he looked down into a crib at a little boy named Methuselah, he began to walk with God. If Methuselah had died in his crib, he would have accomplished about as much as evidently he did in his long life.

Your little one served its purpose. A brief life is not an incomplete life.*

---

* J. Vernon McGee, *Death of a Little Child* (Glendale, Calif.: Griffin, 1984), 10–11.

While I saw Corey's death as a life cut short, perhaps God considered Corey's life and death as a job completed. Though I didn't understand it, I began to see that whatever Corey's purpose in life had been, it had been completed in the fourteen months he was here.

Many people were praying for us, but I couldn't pray for myself. Spiritually I was sick. I didn't know what to believe about God anymore, yet I could sense the presence of the Holy Spirit hovering over me in much the same way I hover over my children when they are ill. Like a loving parent, He stayed close to me, tried to comfort me, and checked on my progress. He was waiting for me to let Him help me, but I refused to be comforted.

I was concerned because Ryan wouldn't talk about Corey's death. Even though I had encouraged Ryan to talk about it, he kept it all inside him. Sometimes when I tucked him in bed at night, he would have tears in his eyes. I knew he was grieving deeply, but he wouldn't open up to me and tell me what was on his mind. My child was in pain but he wouldn't let me help him. I thought, *My precious child, I know you are in pain. If you would tell me how you feel, I could help you through this. I will help you carry your burden. Tell me of your feelings of fear, anger, and pain. I'm waiting and wanting to help you, but you must let me help you, all you have to do is ask.*

Then I heard the still, small voice deep within me say, "Carla, don't you see this is the same thing you are doing? My precious child, I know you are in pain. If you would tell me how you feel, I could help you through this. I will help you carry your burden. Tell me of your feelings of fear, anger, and pain. I'm waiting and wanting to help you, but you must let me help you. All you have to do is ask."

A member of a local church that sponsors Mother's Day Out, a weekly babysitting service, called to see if I wanted to enroll Brittney. I did. I had tried to get both Brittney and Corey enrolled, but Corey's class was full.

Both of them had gone before on days when there was a place open in both classes. It made me sick to think that with Corey gone, there wasn't a problem getting Brittney in.

The first day I took Brittney without Corey I thought I would die. I got only one child out of the car, walked in with empty arms that ached to hold my son, carried just one lunch box, and paid for one child. I reached my car before collapsing into a heap of sobbing pain. When I could drive, I drove to the cemetery to visit Corey's grave. Fresh dirt and a little sign from the funeral home marked the place that held my son's precious body. I had no tears left in me to shed. I stood like a zombie and thought about the class of toddlers at Mother's Day Out. Corey had been in the class with those same toddlers and teachers only a few weeks before. Now his body was lying in a cold grave while the other children played. I wondered, *How will I live without him?*

The house was silent when I returned. I felt I could not live one more hour without Corey. For the first time since Corey died, I fell to my knees and poured out my rage to God. I told him how I honestly felt. I cried and screamed my way through every bitter thought and emotion, regardless of how blasphemous it was. I honestly told God the feelings I had. When I was through venting my rage, I asked God to give me peace in my heart to make it through the next hour. For the first time in my life I experienced the peace of God spoken of in the Bible. "The peace of God, which surpasses all understanding, will guard your hearts and minds through Christ Jesus" (Philippians 4:7).

Neither the sorrow nor the pain was gone, but the divine peace only God can give was mine when I asked for it. God didn't strike me down with a bolt of lightning when I railed at Him, He brought me peace. I found He loved me most when I deserved it the least.

Time after time when I felt I couldn't go on, I would be honest with God about my feelings and ask for His help to get through it. I learned that when I needed help, I was responsible to reach out for it. Asking Him for peace and strength when I needed it, He never failed to supply it. I would sometimes doubt I could survive the rest of the day, and couldn't even think about tomorrow.

God taught me I had to depend on Him daily. When the children of Israel were in the wilderness, God supplied manna one day at a time. They couldn't gather one day what they needed for the next, except on the day before the Sabbath. So it was with me: God didn't give me today the strength to face tomorrow. I had to depend on Him one day at a time. He supplied me with the strength to get through each day just when I needed it. When tomorrow came, He supplied my needs again.

It seemed that every step I made toward God was countered by the devil, who redoubled his efforts to keep me bitter. Questions and doubts were always on my mind. I continued to struggle with the question of why God allowed Corey to die. I wanted to find a reason that would justify his death in my mind. I thought if a member of my family had turned to Jesus for salvation at last after this tragedy, then perhaps I could accept it, but that didn't happen.

Could there be a reason good enough for me to understand why he died and think it was worth the price? No, I knew in my heart I would never sacrifice my son for anyone or anything. I knew that I would sacrifice my own life for the lives of my children, but I would never sacrifice my child's life for anyone. It was then the still, small voice within me said, "Carla, you wouldn't be willing to sacrifice your son, but I was willing to sacrifice mine. I could have saved my Son from death on the cross, but I allowed Him to die so that your son might have eternal life."

For the first time I understood the depth of love God has for humankind. He allowed His sinless son, Jesus, to die a humiliating, painful death on the cross so that all who believe in Him could have eternal life. God didn't sacrifice His son only for good people, He sacrificed His son because He loved all people, even murderers, thieves, rapists, and child molesters. While I wouldn't sacrifice my son for anyone, God sacrificed His son for everyone. The magnitude of His love is beyond my understanding.

How could I ever understand the ways of God? I realized in this life, I would not know or understand why God allowed Corey to die. Somehow, when I accepted the fact that I would never know, I was able to stop searching for the answer.

Chapter 14

WHILE I BEGAN TO PRAY when I needed strength and comfort, I continued to struggle with bitterness and anger toward God. I had a husband, and we still had two children to raise. I knew if I didn't make peace with God, I would never be a whole person again. I couldn't be the kind of wife and mother I wanted to be and feel the way I did. I turned to the Bible to see if I could work through my chaotic feelings.

I turned first to the book of Job. How did a parent handle losing all ten of his children, and his health, and his wealth and be remembered for his patience? Though I had heard Bible lessons about Job before, I was studying it now from a much different viewpoint. It was as if I had never heard it before.

At the beginning, Job says, " 'Shall we indeed accept good from God, and shall we not accept adversity?' In all this Job did not sin with his lips" (Job 2:10). What an amazing thing to say after all he had been through. At the time, Job was covered head to toe with boils; he had lost his servants, livestock, and all ten of his children.

It was the attitude Job came to have later that I could identify with. Job's three friends came and sat with Job in silence for a week, his grief was so deep. When Job speaks again, he wishes he had never been born. He ends this speech by saying, "My sighing comes before I eat, and my groanings pour out like water. For the thing I greatly feared has come upon me, and what I dreaded has happened to me. I am not at ease, nor am I quiet; I have no rest, for trouble comes" (Job 3:24–26).

I was consumed day and night by the thought that I will not see Corey again on this side of eternity. I can never hold him in my arms again no matter how they ache to touch him. I understood Job when he said, "When I lie down, I say, 'When shall I arise, and the night be ended? For I have had my fill of tossing till dawn' " (Job 7:4).

As the book of Job progresses, his friends are sure Job is being punished for some hidden sin, and they encourage him to confess. Job insists he is innocent and wishes he could argue his case before God. Job says, "Even today my complaint is bitter; my hand is listless because of my groaning. Oh, that I knew where I might find Him; that I might come to His seat! I would present my case before Him, and fill my mouth with arguments. I would know the words which He would answer me, and understand what He would say to me" (Job 23:2–5). Many centuries of time separate Job and me, yet from his words, I knew I was feeling the same sense of injustice and anger he felt.

Job speaks of being abandoned by God, "I cry out to You, but You do not answer me; I stand up, and You regard me. But You have become cruel to me; with the strength of Your hand You oppose me" (Job 30:20–21). I had tried to live my life pleasing to God while many around me lived without regard for Him. Yet when trouble came, it came to me, not to them. Like Job, I felt I could argue my case before God and show Him I didn't deserve such treatment.

God responds to Job in chapters 38–41. Although the words were spoken to Job, God was giving the same message to me as I read them. God Almighty spoke out of a whirlwind and told Job and me, "Who is this who darkens counsel by words without knowledge? Now prepare yourself like a man; I will question you, and you shall answer Me. Where were you when I laid the foundations of the earth? Tell Me, if you have understanding" (Job 38:2–4).

God continues with examples of His almighty power and asks Job, "Shall the one who contends with the Almighty correct Him? He who rebukes God, let him answer it" (Job 40:2).

Job answers God by saying, "Behold, I am vile; what shall I answer You? I lay my hand over my mouth" (Job 40:4–5).

Job was humbled but God wasn't finished with him yet. God asks Job, "Would you indeed annul My judgment? Would you condemn Me that you may be justified?" (Job 40:8).

When God had finished speaking, Job said, "I know that You can do everything, and that no purpose of Yours can be withheld from You. You asked, 'Who is this who hides counsel without knowledge?' Therefore I have uttered what I did not understand, things too wonderful for me, which I did not know" (Job 42:2–3).

Job finishes by saying, "I abhor myself, and repent in dust and ashes" (Job 42:6).

God wanted Job, and me, to learn that God Almighty alone created the earth and all in it. All things are His to do with as He sees fit. It is not my place to question or argue with God. The judgments God makes are His alone to make.

The lesson I learned from Job isn't an easy one. It doesn't fit in with my human way of thinking, or my sense of justice. It may not be my way, but it is God's way. We are the creation while God is the Creator.

Chapter 15

I SEEMED TO HAVE MORE QUESTIONS than answers about God and how He works. How could a loving God allow my son to die? If God is in control of everything, what was the difference between God's allowing Corey's death and His taking Corey's life? I began to pray not only for strength and comfort, but for wisdom in how to look at the circumstances of my life. I wanted the wisdom spoken of in the book of James: "If any of you lacks wisdom, let him ask of God, who gives to all liberally and without reproach, and it will be given to him" (James 1:5).

I wanted to understand what Romans 8:28 meant. It says, "We know that all things work together for good to those who love God, to those who are the called according to His purpose." I could not believe God thought the death of my son was good. There was nothing good in the way I felt about it. My faith was shattered, how could that be good? I began to study and pray for wisdom about it. I learned this verse doesn't say that everything that happens is good, it says all things can work together for good. For those people who love God and are living according to His purpose, anything that happens can be used of God to further His purpose.

An example of this is the life of Joseph in the book of Genesis. Many things that happened in Joseph's life were not good. He was sold by his brothers into slavery in Egypt, and was unjustly put in prison for years. Through all these things, God was in control. Since Joseph was living his life according to God's purpose, God could use even the bad things in his life to bring about good for others. God allowed Joseph to rise to the position of power in Egypt so he would be in a position to save his family from starvation when the famine came. Joseph probably didn't realize when he was a slave or in prison that God was using the situation for good. But God knew that the family Joseph would save from starving was the same family whom He had chosen as the human family for His son, Jesus, many years later.

God showed me through these passages that even when something bad happens in my life, He can use it for a greater good, if I let Him. Even when I don't understand how or why.

One day I read the account in Matthew 14:22–32 where Peter walked on the water. After feeding the five thousand, Jesus told His disciples to take a boat and go to the other side of the Sea of Galilee. Jesus went up the mountain alone to pray. A storm blew up during the night and caused the ship to be tossed about on the waves of the sea. Jesus walked on the sea toward the ship. When the disciples saw Him, they were afraid, but Jesus said, "Be of good cheer! It is I; do not be afraid."

Peter said, "Lord, if it is You, command me to come to You on the water."

Jesus said, "Come."

Peter got out of the ship and walked on the water toward Jesus. This ordinary man was actually walking on water. Then, Peter must have thought, *I can't do this!* He looked around, saw the strong wind, and grew afraid. Only then did he start sinking. He cried to Jesus, "Lord, save me!"

Jesus reached for Peter, caught him, and said, "O you of little faith, why did you doubt?" The wind stopped when Jesus and Peter got into the ship.

Even though I had read these verses many times through the years, suddenly I knew the lesson God was showing me through this passage. If I keep my eyes on Jesus, I can walk through this storm of grief and sorrow my life had become. With Jesus, I can stay above the churning sea of doubt and uncertainty. But when I take my eyes away from Jesus and look at the circumstances of my life, I begin to sink back into the sea of fear, anger, and doubt. I had a choice to make: either walk with Jesus through the storm, or be swallowed up by it. It was up to me. Again the words of the hymn sang in my mind:

Turn your eyes upon Jesus,
Look full in His wonderful face:
And the things of earth will grow
    strangely dim
In the light of His glory and grace.[*]

Chapter 16

I COULDN'T FORGET THE DESPERATE PRAYERS I prayed while Corey was in the hospital. Why didn't God answer my prayers to spare Corey's life? I prayed in faith believing that God would answer them. What went wrong? Is "no" sometimes God's answer to prayer? I searched to see if the Bible recorded any prayers that were answered "no." I found the following:

- Moses prays for his own death (Numbers 11:15).
- Moses asks to go over the Jordan river into the Promised Land (Deuteronomy 3:24–25).

- David prays for his sick infant (2 Samuel 12:16, 18).
- Elijah prays for his own death (1 Kings 19:4).
- Jonah prays for his own death (Jonah 4:3).
- Paul prays for God to remove the thorn in his flesh (2 Corinthians 12:7–10).
- Jesus prays before His arrest and crucifixion that the cup might pass from Him (Matthew 26:36–46; Mark 14:32–42; Luke 22:39–46).

I studied the principles of prayer in the Bible. I found prayer to be more than just asking for what we want. The Bible gives several reasons why our prayers may be hindered:

- Selfishness (Proverbs 21:13; James 4:3).
- Strife within a marriage (1 Peter 3:7).
- An unforgiving attitude (Mark 11:25–26).
- Unbelief (James 1:6–7).
- Unconfessed sin (Psalm 66:18; Isaiah 59:2).

- Praying outside the will of God (1 John 5:14–15).
- Lack of compassion (Proverbs 21:13).

The Bible gives us some guidelines about how we are to pray:

- We are to pray to God the Father (Matthew 6:9).
- Through the Holy Spirit (Romans 8:26–27; Ephesians 6:18; Jude 20).
- In the name of Jesus (John 14:13–14).

These verses teach me I should be guided by the Holy Spirit in what to pray to God about, then ask for those things in Jesus' name. When I end my prayers with "in Jesus name" it is as though I were saying, "These are the things for which Jesus Himself would have prayed in the same circumstances."

I realized many of my prayers were not what Jesus would have prayed. For when Jesus prayed, above all He wanted the will of His Father to be done.

I studied the prayers of Jesus in the Garden of Gethsemane. Jesus knew the time had come for His arrest and crucifixion. He knew Judas was in the act of betraying Him. He had a heavy, sorrowful heart and asked Peter, James, and John to stay up and watch with Him. Jesus prayed, "O My Father, if it is possible, let this cup pass from Me; nevertheless, not as I will, but as You will" (Matthew 26:39).

When He came back to the disciples, He found them sleeping. His beloved disciples wouldn't even stay awake and watch with Him as He prayed. As they slept, Jesus prayed this same prayer two more times. It was here that God answered "no," even to His own perfect Son.

Whatever the cost to Himself, Jesus wanted to do God's will, not His own. Jesus accepted the will of His Father and faced the mob as they entered the garden to arrest Him.

Jesus taught me in these beautiful verses that above all, I should want the will of God. Even when it conflicts with what I want.

Had I misunderstood the function of prayer? Was I using prayer only as a way to get things from God? I learned that prayer is not meant to change God, but to change me. My will needs to be brought in line with God's will, not the other way around. If God's own Son bowed to the Father's will in all things, shouldn't I?

If I seek God's will in all things and not my own desires, then I will ask for only those things that are within God's will. Then I can be assured my prayers will be answered. "This is the confidence that we have in Him, that if we ask anything according to His will, He hears us. And if we know that He hears us, whatever we ask, we know that we have the petitions that we have asked of Him" (1 John 5:14–15).

Chapter 17

FOR EVERY DAY I FELT STRONG in the Lord, I had two of doubt and bitterness. I wondered how I could be filled with the peace of God one day, and the next day be bitter and confused again. No one could understand how I felt. While one person couldn't understand my faith in God, another couldn't understand my doubts.

I prayed, *God, I'm still so confused. What I know to be true one day is what I doubt the next. Give me your wisdom to see things the way you want me to see them.*

One day when I was feeling particularly low, I felt compelled to call a friend of mine who was experiencing some personal problems. As she spoke about her problems and feelings, a Scripture verse would come to my mind that I felt would guide or comfort her. Again and again I shared Scripture verses with her that I thought would help. When I got off the phone, I was surprised at the way the Bible passages had come to me with perfect clarity. I had never shared Scripture verses with anyone like that before. Then I heard the still, small voice of God speak to my heart saying, *Don't you see my dear child, you are not as confused as you think you are.* I had called with the intention of helping her, but that was not the result. God used our conversation to encourage me.

God gave me a beautiful gift that day. With gentleness He showed me that His words and truth were still the foundation of my soul. The foundation was solid but some days it was so covered with grief I couldn't stand up on it; I had to fall to my knees. He showed me in an unexpected way that underneath it all, I wasn't as confused as I'd thought.

God led me to a passage in Psalms that assured me that even when no one else understood how I felt, He did. "O LORD, You have searched me and known me. You know my sitting down and my rising up; You understand my thought afar off. You comprehend my path and my lying down, and are acquainted with all my ways. For there is not a word on my tongue, but, behold, O LORD, You know it altogether" (Psalm 139:1–4). It comforted me to know that God understood my thoughts even when I didn't understand them myself.

Though many of the Psalms are songs of praise, the ones that helped me most were the ones where the psalmist cried out to God in pain and anguish. My thoughts were so often reflected in his words. "Will the Lord cast off forever? And will He be favorable no more? Has His mercy ceased forever? Has His promise failed forevermore? Has God forgotten to be gracious? Has He in anger shut up His tender mercies?" (Psalm 77:7–9). In this passage, the writer wonders why God has abandoned him. He pours out his feelings, then stops and considers what he has said. The passage continues, "I said, 'This is my anguish; but I will remember the years of the right hand of the Most High.' I will remember the works of the LORD; surely I will remember Your wonders of old. I will also meditate on all Your work, and talk of Your deeds" (Psalm 77:10–12).

The psalmist reached a turning point where he deliberately chooses to remember how God had always been there. When trouble came, he must have felt God had abandoned him just as I did.

In these words I saw that in the worst of times I must turn away from my weakness and choose to worship God. If I let Him, God can take my misery and pain and turn it into a song of praise. He can take the pieces of my broken life and put them back together into a new life.

I realized Jesus was my Savior but not the Lord of my life. I hadn't given Him total control of my life. For Jesus to be my Lord, I must want God's will more than my own. I must seek what I can do for God rather than what God can do for me. I must serve God because I love Him, not because I need Him.

When God's answer to my prayer to save Corey's life was "no," I felt that God had let me down in a way I could never forgive. My joy in this world and my confidence in God was shattered. But, piece by piece, God put my broken spirit back together. God taught me that trusting Him should not depend on the circumstances of my life. The only thing I will take into eternity is my relationship with God. My health may fail, my possessions may vanish, and my family may die. When everything is gone and I've come to the end of my strength, the end of myself, God is there.

Do you feel shattered in spirit and deserted by God? Maybe your burden isn't the death of a loved one; maybe it's sickness, problems with your marriage or children, financial distress, guilt, or depression. God knows all about them. He knows how you feel and why. He wants to help you. He wants to draw you to Himself and give you the strength to face each day. Let Him.

To have real peace with God, you need Jesus as your personal Savior. The Bible says, "If you confess with your mouth the Lord Jesus and believe in your heart that God has raised Him from the dead, you will be saved" (Romans 10:9).

If you are a child of God who is battling anger and resentment, confess your true feelings to Him, and pray for wisdom. No matter how distant God seems, He is there, waiting for you to reach out to Him. God does not change; we do. What has happened in the past can't be changed, but you can change your attitude toward the future.

I learned that God is sovereign. In His divine authority, God doesn't always answer our prayers the way we want Him to. Sometimes, God doesn't change our circumstances, He changes us in our circumstances.

Scriptures That Comfort

From there you will seek the LORD your God, and you will find Him if you seek Him with all your heart and with all your soul. When you are in distress, and all these things come upon you in the latter days, when you turn to the LORD your God and obey His voice (for the LORD your God is a merciful God), He will not forsake you nor destroy you, nor forget the covenant of your fathers which He swore to them.

Deuteronomy 4:29–31

You, O LORD, are a shield for me, my glory and the One who lifts up my head.

Psalm 3:3

I lay down and slept; I awoke, for the LORD sustained me.

Psalm 3:5

I will both lie down in peace, and sleep; for You alone, O LORD, make me dwell in safety.

Psalm 4:8

You, O LORD, will bless the righteous; with favor You will surround him as with a shield.

Psalm 5:12

Have mercy on me, O LORD, for I am weak; O LORD, heal me, for my bones are troubled. My soul also is greatly troubled; but You, O LORD—how long?

Return, O LORD, deliver me! Oh, save me for Your mercies' sake! For in death there is no remembrance of You; in the grave who will give You thanks?

I am weary with my groaning; all night I make my bed swim; I drench my couch with my tears. My eye wastes away because of grief; it grows old because of all my enemies.

Depart from me, all you workers of iniquity; for the LORD has heard the voice of my weeping. The LORD has heard my supplication; the LORD will receive my prayer.

Psalm 6:2–9

Those who know Your name will put their trust in You; for You, LORD, have not forsaken those who seek You.

Psalm 9:10

Show Your marvelous lovingkindness by Your right hand, O You who save those who trust in You from those who rise up against them. Keep me as the apple of Your eye; hide me under the shadow of Your wings.

Psalm 17:7–8

GOD

I will love You, O LORD, my strength. The LORD is my rock and my fortress and my deliverer; my God, my strength, in whom I will trust; my shield and the horn of my salvation, my stronghold.

Psalm 18:1–2

In my distress I called upon the LORD, and cried out to my God; He heard my voice from His temple, and my cry came before Him, even to His ears.

Psalm 18:6

Turn Yourself to me, and have mercy on me, for I am desolate and afflicted. The troubles of my heart have enlarged; bring me out of my distresses! Look on my affliction and my pain, and forgive all my sins.

Psalm 25:16–18

Let integrity and uprightness preserve me, for I wait for You.

Psalm 25:21

The LORD is my light and my salvation; whom shall I fear? The LORD is the strength of my life; of whom shall I be afraid?

Psalm 27:1

In the time of trouble He shall hide me in His pavilion; in the secret place of His tabernacle He shall hide me; He shall set me high upon a rock.

Psalm 27:5

Wait on the LORD; be of good courage, and He shall strengthen your heart; wait, I say, on the LORD!

Psalm 27:14

The LORD is my strength and my shield; my heart trusted in Him, and I am helped; therefore my heart greatly rejoices, and with my song I will praise Him.

Psalm 28:7

Bow down Your ear to me, deliver me speedily; be my rock of refuge, a fortress of defense to save me. For You are my rock and my fortress; therefore, for Your name's sake, lead me and guide me.

Psalm 31:2–3

I will be glad and rejoice in Your mercy, for You have considered my trouble; You have known my soul in adversities.

Psalm 31:7

Have mercy on me, O LORD, for I am in trouble; my eye wastes away with grief, yes, my soul and my body! For my life is spent with grief, and my years with sighing; my strength fails because of my iniquity, and my bones waste away.

Psalm 31:9–10

Be of good courage, and He shall strengthen your heart, all you who hope in the LORD.

Psalm 31:24

GOD

I sought the LORD, and He heard me, and delivered me from all my fears.

Psalm 34:4

This poor man cried out, and the LORD heard him, and saved him out of all his troubles. The angel of the LORD encamps all around those who fear Him, and delivers them.

Psalm 34:6–7

The righteous cry out, and the LORD hears, and delivers them out of all their troubles. The LORD is near to those who have a broken heart, and saves such as have a contrite spirit. Many are the afflictions of the righteous, but the LORD delivers him out of them all.

Psalm 34:17–19

The steps of a good man are ordered by the LORD, and He delights in his way. Though he fall, he shall not be utterly cast down; for the LORD upholds him with His hand.

Psalm 37:23–24

The salvation of the righteous is from the LORD; He is their strength in the time of trouble, and the LORD shall help them and deliver them; He shall deliver them from the wicked, and save them, because they trust in Him.

Psalm 37:39–40

I waited patiently for the LORD; and He inclined to me, and heard my cry. He also brought me up out of a horrible pit, out of the miry clay, and set my feet upon a rock, and established my steps. He has put a new song in my mouth—praise to our God; many will see it and fear, and will trust in the LORD.

Blessed is that man who makes the LORD his trust, and does not respect the proud, nor such as turn aside to lies. Many, O LORD my God, are Your wonderful works which You have done; and Your thoughts toward us cannot be recounted to You in order; if I would declare and speak of them, they are more than can be numbered.

Psalm 40:1–5

I am poor and needy; yet the LORD thinks upon me. You are my help and my deliverer; do not delay, O my God.

Psalm 40:17

Why are you cast down, O my soul? And why are you disquieted within me? Hope in God; for I shall yet praise Him, the help of my countenance and my God.

Psalm 43:5

God is our refuge and strength, a very present help in trouble. Therefore we will not fear, even though the earth be removed, and though the mountains be carried into the midst of the sea; though its waters roar and be troubled, though the mountains shake with its swelling. Selah.

Psalm 46:1–3

Call upon Me in the day of trouble; I will deliver you, and you shall glorify Me.

Psalm 50:15

As for me, I will call upon God, and the LORD shall save me. Evening and morning and at noon I will pray, and cry aloud, and He shall hear my voice.

Psalm 55:16–17

Cast your burden on the LORD, and He shall sustain you; He shall never permit the righteous to be moved.

Psalm 55:22

Whenever I am afraid, I will trust in You. In God (I will praise His word), in God I have put my trust; I will not fear, what can flesh do to me?

Psalm 56:3–4

You number my wanderings; put my tears into Your bottle; are they not in Your book?

Psalm 56:8

In God I have put my trust; I will not be afraid. What can man do to me?

Psalm 56:11

Be merciful to me, O God, be merciful to me! For my soul trusts in You; and in the shadow of Your wings I will make my refuge, until these calamities have passed by. I will cry out to God Most High, to God who performs all things for me.

Psalm 57:1–2

I will sing of Your power; yes, I will sing aloud of Your mercy in the morning; for You have been my defense and refuge in the day of my trouble. To You, O my Strength, I will sing praises; for God is my defense, my God of mercy.

Psalm 59:16–17

Hear my cry, O God; attend to my prayer. From the end of the earth I will cry to You, when my heart is overwhelmed; lead me to the rock that is higher than I.

For You have been a shelter for me, a strong tower from the enemy. I will abide in Your tabernacle forever; I will trust in the shelter of Your wings. Selah.

Psalm 61:1–4

Truly my soul silently waits for God; from Him comes my salvation. He alone is my rock and my salvation; He is my defense; I shall not be greatly moved.

Psalm 62:1–2

My soul, wait silently for God alone, for my expectation is from Him. He only is my rock and my salvation; He is my defense; I shall not be moved. In God is my salvation and my glory; the rock of my strength, and my refuge, is in God.

Trust in Him at all times, you people; pour out your heart before Him; God is a refuge for us. Selah.

Psalm 62:5–8

When I remember You on my bed, I meditate on You in the night watches. Because You have been my help, therefore in the shadow of Your wings I will rejoice. My soul follows close behind You; Your right hand upholds me.

Psalm 63:6–8

Save me, O God! For the waters have come up to my neck. I sink in deep mire, where there is no standing; I have come into deep waters, where the floods overflow me. I am weary with my crying; my throat is dry; my eyes fail while I wait for my God.

Psalm 69:1–3

Deliver me out of the mire, and let me not sink; let me be delivered from those who hate me, and out of the deep waters. Let not the floodwater overflow me, nor let the deep swallow me up; and let not the pit shut its mouth on me.

Hear me, O LORD, for Your lovingkindness is good; turn to me according to the multitude of Your tender mercies. And do not hide Your face from Your servant, for I am in trouble; hear me speedily.

Psalm 69:14–17

I am poor and sorrowful; let Your salvation, O God, set me up on high. I will praise the name of God with a song, and will magnify Him with thanksgiving.

Psalm 69:29–30

Let all those who seek You rejoice and be glad in You; and let those who love Your salvation say continually, "Let

God be magnified!" But I am poor and needy; make haste to me, O God! You are my help and my deliverer; O LORD, do not delay.

Psalm 70:4–5

In You, O LORD, I put my trust; let me never be put to shame. Deliver me in Your righteousness, and cause me to escape; incline Your ear to me, and save me. Be my strong refuge, to which I may resort continually; You have given the commandment to save me, for You are my rock and my fortress.

Psalm 71:1–3

My flesh and my heart fail; but God is the strength of my heart and my portion forever.

Psalm 73:26

It is good for me to draw near to God; I have put my trust in the Lord GOD, that I may declare all Your works.

Psalm 73:28

Be merciful to me, O Lord, for I cry to You all day long.

Psalm 86:3

In the day of my trouble I will call upon You, for you will answer me.

Psalm 86:7

You, O Lord, are a God full of compassion, and gracious, longsuffering and abundant in mercy and truth.

GOD

Oh, turn to me, and have mercy on me! Give Your strength to Your servant, and save the son of Your maidservant. Show me a sign for good, that those who hate me may see it and be ashamed, because You, LORD, have helped me and comforted me.

Psalm 86:15–17

I will say of the LORD, "He is my refuge and my fortress; My God, in Him I will trust."

Psalm 91:2

He shall cover you with His feathers, and under His wings you shall take refuge; His truth shall be your shield and buckler.

Psalm 91:4

Unless the LORD had been my help, my soul would soon have settled in silence. If I say, "My foot slips," Your mercy, O LORD, will hold me up. In the multitude of my anxieties within me, Your comforts delight my soul.

Psalm 94:17–19

The LORD has been my defense, and my God the rock of my refuge.

Psalm 94:22

You, O GOD the Lord, deal with me for Your name's sake; because Your mercy is good, deliver me. For I am poor and needy, and my heart is wounded within me. I am gone like a shadow when it lengthens; I am shaken off like a locust. My knees are weak through fasting, and my flesh is feeble from lack of fatness. I also have become a reproach to them; when they look at me, they shake their heads.

Help me, O LORD my God! Oh, save me according to Your mercy, that they may know that this is Your hand—that You, LORD, have done it!

Psalm 109:21–27

I love the LORD, because He has heard my voice and my supplications. Because He has inclined His ear to me, therefore I will call upon Him as long as I live.

The pains of death surrounded me, and the pangs of Sheol laid hold of me; I found trouble and sorrow. Then I called upon the name of the LORD: "O LORD, I implore You, deliver my soul!"

Gracious is the LORD, and righteous; yes, our God is merciful. The LORD preserves the simple; I was brought low, and He saved me. Return to your rest, O my soul, for the LORD has dealt bountifully with you.

For You have delivered my soul from death, my eyes from tears, and my feet from falling. I will walk before the LORD in the land of the living.

Psalm 116:1–9

Precious in the sight of the LORD is the death of His saints.

Psalm 116:15

———

GOD

I called on the LORD in distress; the LORD answered me and set me in a broad place. The LORD is on my side; I will not fear. What can man do to me? The LORD is for me among those who help me; therefore I shall see my desire on those who hate me. It is better to trust in the LORD than to put confidence in man. It is better to trust in the LORD than to put confidence in princes.

Psalm 118:5–9

The LORD is my strength and song, and He has become my salvation.

Psalm 118:14

Make me understand the way of Your precepts; so shall I meditate on Your wonderful works. My soul melts from heaviness; strengthen me according to Your word.

Psalm 119:27–28

You are my hiding place and my shield; I hope in Your word.

Psalm 119:114

Trouble and anguish have overtaken me, yet Your commandments are my delights.

Psalm 119:143

I will lift up my eyes to the hills—from whence comes my help? My help comes from the LORD, who made heaven and earth.

He will not allow your foot to be moved; He who keeps you will not slumber. Behold, He who keeps Israel shall neither slumber nor sleep.

The LORD is your keeper; the LORD is your shade at your right hand.

Psalm 121:1–5

In the day when I cried out, You answered me, and made me bold with strength in my soul.

Psalm 138:3

O LORD, You have searched me and known me. You know my sitting down and my rising up; You understand my thought afar off. You comprehend my path and my lying down, and are acquainted with all my ways. For there is not a word on my tongue, but behold, O LORD, You know it altogether. You have hedged me behind and before, and laid Your hand upon me. Such knowledge is too wonderful for me; it is high, I cannot attain it.

Where can I go from Your Spirit? Or where can I flee from Your presence? If I ascend into heaven, You are there; if I make my bed in hell, behold, You are there. If I take the wings of the morning, and dwell in the uttermost parts of the sea, even there Your hand shall lead me, and Your right hand shall hold me. If I say, "Surely the darkness shall fall on me," even the night shall be light about me; indeed, the darkness shall not hide from You, but the night shines as the day; the darkness and the light are both alike to You.

For you formed my inward parts; You covered me in my mother's womb. I will praise You, for I am fearfully and wonderfully made; marvelous are Your works, and that my soul knows very well.

My frame was not hidden from You, when I was made in secret, and skillfully wrought in the lowest parts of the earth. Your eyes saw my substance, being yet unformed. And in Your book they all were written, the days fashioned for me, when as yet there were none of them.

How precious also are Your thoughts to me, O God! How great is the sum of them! If I should count them, they would be more in number than the sand; when I awake, I am still with You.

Psalm 139:1–18

I cry out to the LORD with my voice; with my voice to the LORD I make my supplication. I pour out my complaint before Him; I declare before Him my trouble.

When my spirit was overwhelmed within me, then You knew my path. In the way in which I walk they have secretly set a snare for me. Look on my right hand and see, for there is no one who acknowledges me; refuge has failed me; no one cares for my soul.

I cried out to You, O LORD: I said, "You are my refuge, my portion in the land of the living. Attend to my cry, for I am brought very low; deliver me from my persecutors, for they are stronger than I. Bring my soul out of prison, that I may praise Your name; the righteous shall surround me, for You shall deal bountifully with me."

Psalm 142:1–7

My spirit is overwhelmed within me; my heart within me is distressed.

I remember the days of old; I meditate on all Your works; I muse on the work of Your hands. I spread out my hands to You; my soul longs for You like a thirsty land. Selah.

Answer me speedily, O LORD; my spirit falls! Do not hide Your face from me, lest I be like those who go down into the pit. Cause me to hear Your lovingkindness in the morning, for in You do I trust; cause me to know the way in which I should walk, for I lift up my soul to You.

Deliver me, O LORD, from my enemies; in You I take shelter. Teach me to do Your will, for You are my God; Your Spirit is good. Lead me in the land of uprightness.

Revive me, O LORD, for Your name's sake! For Your righteousness' sake to bring my soul out of trouble.

Psalm 143:4–11

The LORD upholds all who fall, and raises up all who are bowed down.

Psalm 145:14

He heals the brokenhearted and binds up their wounds. He counts the number of the stars; He calls them all by name. Great is our Lord, and mighty in power; His understanding is infinite.

Psalm 147:3–5

My son, if you receive my words, and treasure my commands within you, so that you incline your ear to wis-

---

dom, and apply your heart to understanding; yes, if you cry out for discernment, and lift up your voice for understanding, if you seek her as silver, and search for her as for hidden treasures; then you will understand the fear of the LORD, and find the knowledge of God. For the LORD gives wisdom; from His mouth come knowledge and understanding; He stores up sound wisdom for the upright; He is a shield to those who walk uprightly; He guards the paths of justice, and preserves the way of His saints.

Proverbs 2:1–8

Trust in the LORD with all your heart, and lean not on your own understanding; in all your ways acknowledge Him, and He shall direct your paths.

Proverbs 3:5–6

He will swallow up death forever, and the Lord GOD will wipe away tears from all faces; the rebuke of His people He will take away from all the earth; for the LORD has spoken.

Isaiah 25:8

And though the Lord gives you the bread of adversity and the water of affliction, yet your teachers will not be moved into a corner anymore, but your eyes shall see your teachers. Your ears shall hear a word behind you, saying, "This is the way, walk in it," whenever you turn to the right hand or whenever you turn to the left.

Isaiah 30:20–21

Have you not known? Have you not heard? The everlasting God, the LORD, the Creator of the ends of the earth, neither faints nor is weary. His understanding is unsearchable. He gives power to the weak, and to those who have no might He increases strength. Even the youths shall faint and be weary, and the young men shall utterly fall, but those who wait on the LORD shall renew their strength; they shall mount up with wings like eagles, they shall run and not be weary, they shall walk and not faint.

Isaiah 40:28–31

"Fear not, for I am with you; be not dismayed, for I am your God. I will strengthen you, yes, I will help you. I will uphold you with My righteous right hand."

Isaiah 41:10

"I, the LORD your God, will hold your right hand, saying to you, 'Fear not, I will help you.' "

Isaiah 41:13

But now, thus says the LORD, who created you, O Jacob, and He who formed you, O Israel: "Fear not, for I have redeemed you; I have called you by your name; you are Mine. When you pass through the waters, I will be with you; and through the rivers, they shall not overflow you. When you walk through the fire, you shall not be burned, nor shall the flame scorch you."

Isaiah 43:1–2

"My thoughts are not your thoughts, nor are your ways My ways," says the LORD. "For as the heavens are higher than the earth, so are My ways higher than your ways, and My thoughts than your thoughts.

"For as the rain comes down, and the snow from heaven, and do not return there, but water the earth, and make it bring forth and bud, that it may give seed to the sower and bread to the eater, so shall My word be that goes forth from My mouth; it shall not return to Me void, but it shall accomplish what I please, and it shall prosper in the thing for which I sent it."

Isaiah 55:8–11

"It shall come to pass that before they call, I will answer; and while they are still speaking, I will hear."

Isaiah 65:24

I know the thoughts that I think toward you, says the LORD, thoughts of peace and not of evil, to give you a future and a hope. Then you will call upon Me and go and pray to me, and I will listen to you. And you will seek Me and find Me, when you search for Me with all your heart.

Jeremiah 29:11–13

Through the LORD's mercies we are not consumed, because His compassions fail not. They are new every morning; great is Your faithfulness. "The LORD is my portion," says my soul, "therefore I hope in Him!" The LORD is good to those who wait for Him, to the soul who seeks Him. It is good that one should hope and wait quietly for the salvation of the LORD.

Lamentations 3:22–26

I will look to the LORD; I will wait for the God of my salvation; my God will hear me.

Micah 7:7

The LORD is good, a stronghold in the day of trouble; and He knows those who trust in Him.

Nahum 1:7

Our light affliction, which is but for a moment, is working for us a far more exceeding and eternal weight of glory, while we do not look at the things which are seen, but at the things which are not seen. For the things which are seen are temporary, but the things which are not seen are eternal.

2 Corinthians 4:17–18

Now may our Lord Jesus Christ Himself, and our God and Father, who has loved us and given us everlasting consolation and good hope by grace, comfort your hearts and establish you in every good word and work.

2 Thessalonians 2:16–17

Now may the Lord of peace Himself give you peace always in every way. The Lord be with you all.

2 Thessalonians 3:16

GOD

God has not given us a spirit of fear, but of power and of love and of a sound mind.

2 Timothy 1:7

Let us therefore come boldly to the throne of grace, that we may obtain mercy and find grace to help in time of need.

Hebrews 4:16

Who, in the days of His flesh, when He had offered up prayers and supplications, with vehement cries and tears to Him who was able to save Him from death, and was heard because of His godly fear.

Hebrews 5:7

May the God of all grace, who called us to His eternal glory by Christ Jesus, after you have suffered a while, perfect, establish, strengthen, and settle you.

1 Peter 5:10

Note to the Reader

The publisher invites you to share your response to the message of this book by writing Discovery House Publishers, P. O. Box 3566, Grand Rapids, MI 49501, U.S.A. or by calling 1-800-653-8333. For information about other Discovery House publications, contact us at the same address and phone number.